RUTH LAW
The Queen of the Air

Billie Holladay Skelley

The Crossing Time Series—Book 2

Ruth Law: The Queen of the Air
Copyright © Billie Holladay Skelley 2016
Goldminds Publishing, LLC. (2016) paperback edition (Amphorae Publishing)
Goldminds Publishing, LLC. (2017) hardcover edition (Amphorae Publishing)
Crossing Time Press (2023)

ISBN 13: 978-1-959489-01-6
Library of Congress Control Number: 2011928604

PUBLISHER'S NOTE
Without limiting the rights under the copyright reserved above, no part of this publication may be reproduced, stored in or introduced into a retrieval system, or transmitted, in any form or by any means (electronic, mechanical, photocopying, recording or otherwise), without the prior written permission of both the copyright owner and the above publisher of this book.

Printed in the United States of America

November 1916

Chicago, Illinois: November 13, 1916

"Miss Law! Ruth Law! Do you have a minute to tell our newspaper readers what you are planning to do?"

"I'm going to try to do something that no one has done before—fly from Chicago to New York City in one day. I want to set the American nonstop flight record and show everyone the **practicality** of women aviators."

"Can you give me some background for our readers, like your full name and the year you were born?"

"My name is Ruth Bancroft Law, and I was born in 1887."

"How long have you been flying?"

"I got my pilot's license in 1912, and I bought my first plane from Orville Wright."

"What other aviation records have you set?"

"Well, I've performed several **acrobatic maneuvers**, including the loop-the-loop, and I set an **altitude** record by flying 11,200 feet."

"Do you really think you will be able to fly from Chicago to New York City? Many people doubt that a woman can make such a long-distance flight."

"Yes, I know there are doubters, but my

attempt has been **sanctioned** by the governing body of American aviation, the Aero Club of America."

"The doubters say a woman cannot withstand the confined, cramped quarters encountered on an airplane. They say a woman would not have the **endurance** to withstand the cold, biting winds hour after hour. Many people believe women don't have the **stamina** to last on such a long journey. They think women can't tolerate the **fatigue** that would accompany such a trip."

"As I said, I know there are doubters, but I believe I can do it."

"Other people say your plane is too small to be capable of making such a distance."

"Well, I did try to purchase a larger plane with a greater fuel **capacity**, but Mr. Curtiss, the **manufacturer**, would not sell me one."

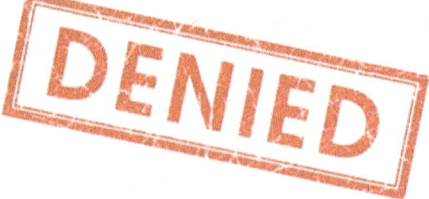

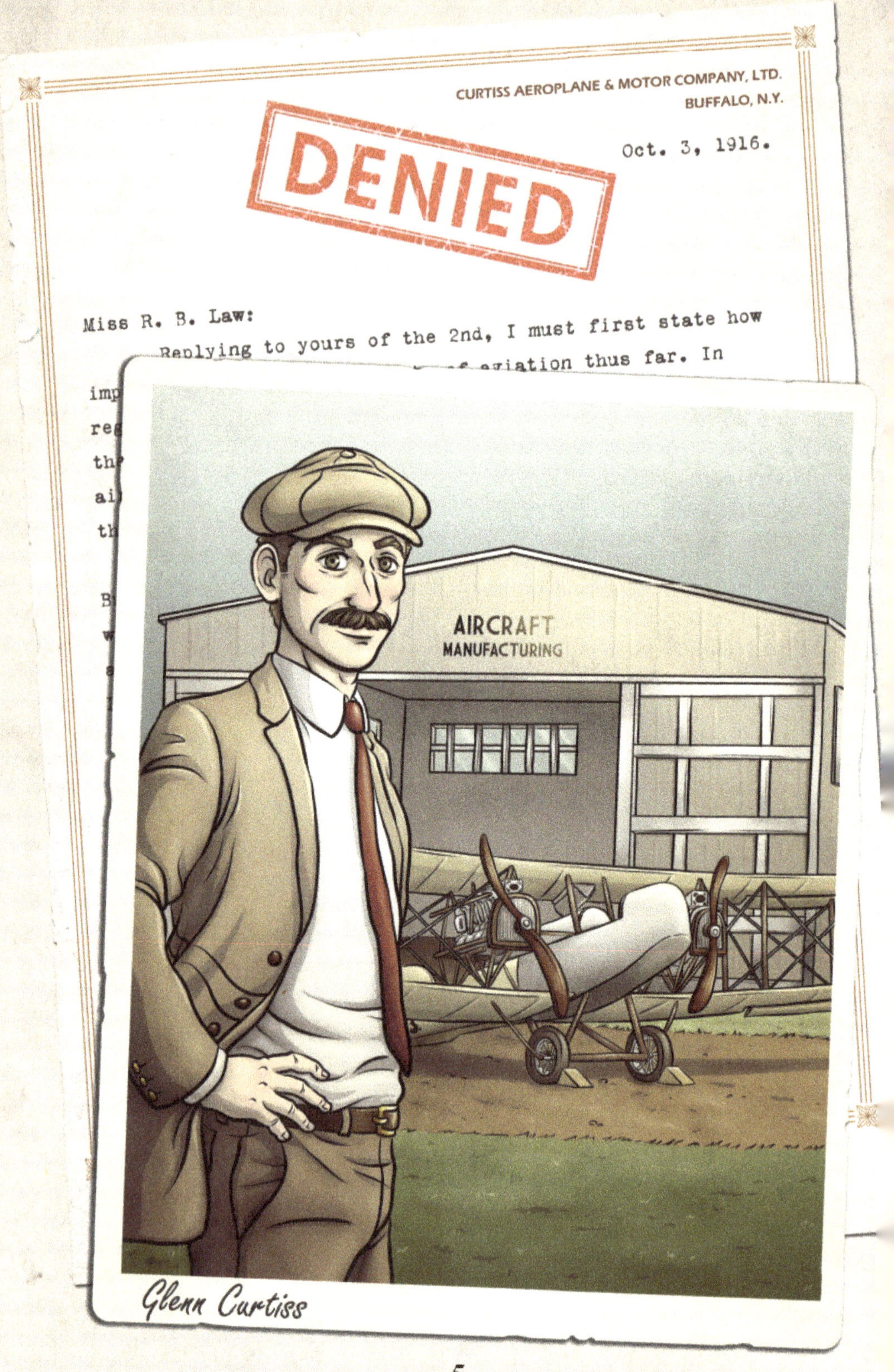
CURTISS AEROPLANE & MOTOR COMPANY, LTD.
BUFFALO, N.Y.
DENIED
Oct. 3, 1916.
Miss R. B. Law:
Replying to yours of the 2nd, I must first state how
aviation thus far. In
AIRCRAFT
MANUFACTURING
Glenn Curtiss

"Why not?"

"He said he was busy making planes for the war effort, and he felt the larger plane was too much for a girl to handle."

"So, what plane are you going to use?"

"I have a Curtiss biplane with an eight-cylinder, hundred-horsepower motor. It has a 12-foot, wood propeller blade in the rear of the plane and a wing spread of 28 feet. The engine is behind the seat which is exposed."

"What do you mean exposed?"

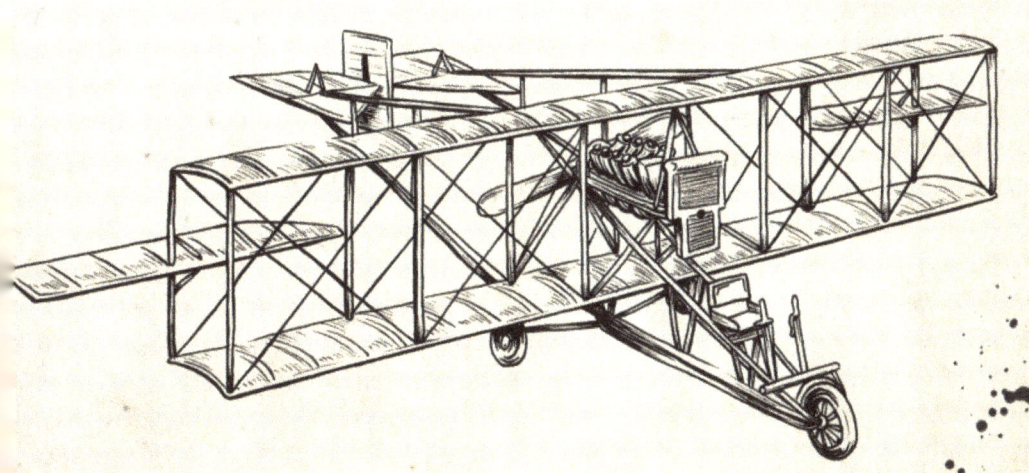

"Well, the pilot's seat is in front of the plane. It has a cushion with a back piece, but the pilot is exposed to the air. You are surrounded on three sides by nothing, and there is no protection from the **elements**."

"What holds you in? I mean what keeps you from falling out?"

"There is a strap that fastens about my waist. It only allows movement of about an inch or two."

"How do you maneuver this aircraft?"

"The **rudders** and controls are manipulated by two levers on either side of the seat. During long flights, the strain on a pilot's arms can be very tiring."

"I can see how it could be physically very wearying, but if your hands are constantly occupied on the controls, how do you check your

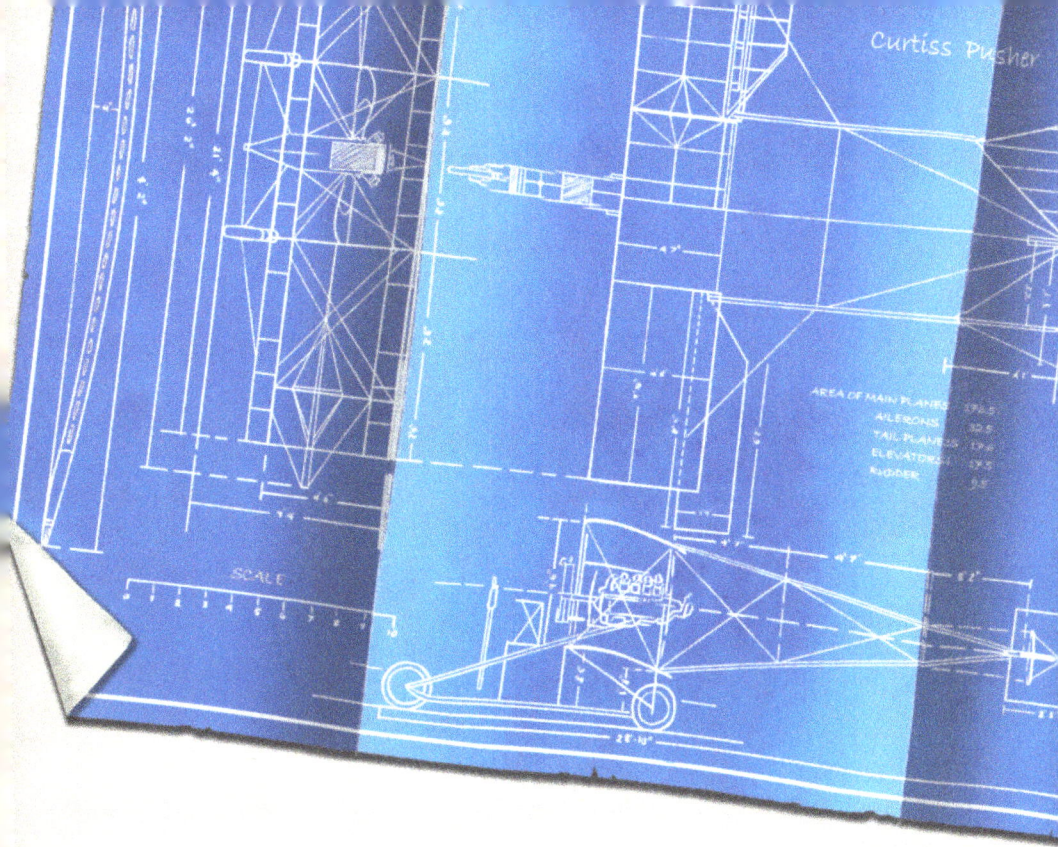

maps and compass readings to see where you are going?"

"I make a list of the compass readings, summarize them in my mind, and then mark the readings on the cuff of my leather **gauntlet**. I map out my projected course and place the scroll of my charts, mounted on rollers, in a case that is strapped to my belt and to the guard on my seat. If I keep my hand on the left control, the **vertical** control, I can use my knee to hold the right control for short periods, so I can wind the knobs of the map case and check my position."

"How do you land this plane?"

"I work the **throttle** with one of my feet and the brake with the other when landing."

"I've actually seen your plane and the hundreds of pieces of piano wire that crisscross your machine. You have to admit that such a

stick-and-wire plane does not look adequate for what you are asking it to do?"

"I know some people think my plane is **obsolete** and **antiquated**, but my little 'pusher' is up to the task."

"Have you made any special preparations for your historic attempt?"

"Well, I've added an extra gas tank. Originally, my plane carried only 16 gallons of gasoline, but with the new tank, the fuel capacity is now 53 gallons. I've also taken all the **surplus** weight off the plane that I can—including the lights."

"In the unprotected seat, how will you tolerate the cold and dampness? I mean won't you be in the numbing cold for hours?"

"I have been trying to condition my body, to prepare it for the cold, by sleeping in a tent

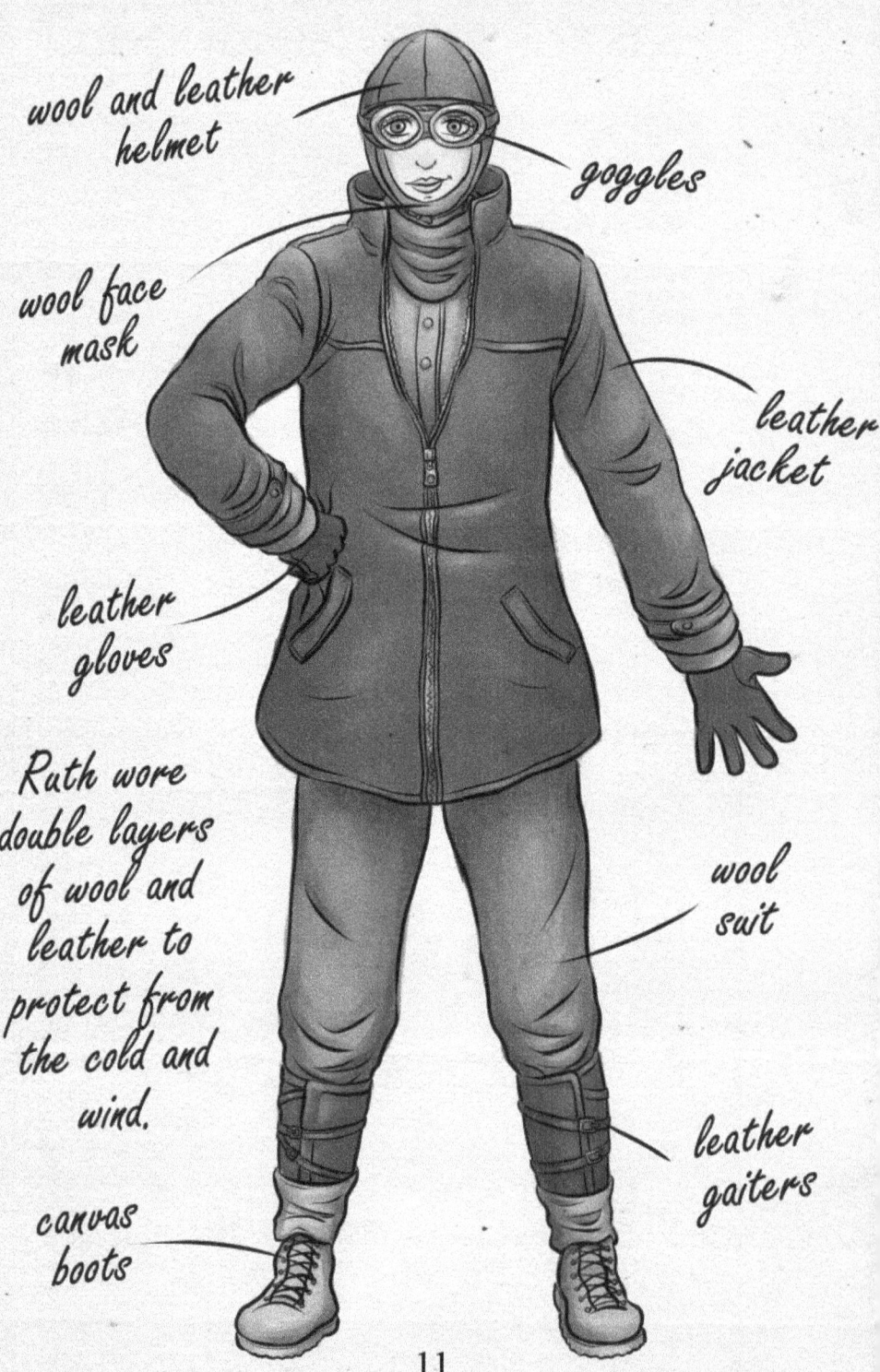

at night on the roof of the Morrison Hotel. At high altitudes, I know it will be very cold. I've also changed my flight **attire**. I will be wearing two wool suits and two leather suits, as well as a leather and wool helmet with a wool face mask, and goggles. The extra layers of

Morrison Hotel

clothing make it difficult to move my arms and complicate handling the controls, but I'll need the extra garments for protection from the cold."

"Will you be carrying anything else on the trip?"

"I have a skirt that I will bring, too. I'll store it behind the seat. When I'm flying it is useless, but when I land, I will put the skirt over my flying attire."

"So, the realities of flying trump the acceptable fashion?"

"Absolutely. I'll wear the skirt in public when I land, but when I'm flying, I dress as a pilot and for the elements."

"Will you be carrying anything else?"

"Just a set of letters for people in New York."

"Thank you, Miss Law. Good luck to you."

Chicago, Illinois: November 19, 1916

"Would you mind telling our newspaper readers why Miss Law was so late taking off?"

"We just had a series of setbacks, one thing after another."

"Are you her mechanic?"

"Yes."

"Well, what happened?"

"It was so cold we couldn't get her engine to start. Her departure was further delayed by a fifty-mile **gale** from the northeast. The winds really picked up just as she was getting ready to fly."

"Excuse me, but are you crying?"

"I was afraid. I was afraid she would be killed."

"Why?"

"There was just this strange **tumult** of **erratic** air currents—fiercely shifting winds with huge gusts when she went to depart. I held my breath because, at first, she could not attain a height of more than 200 feet. I was afraid she might not clear the buildings. I was afraid there was going to be a **catastrophe**."

"But she did take off?"

"Yes, she has tremendous flying skill and she is extremely determined. She left from Grant Park, on the shore of Lake Michigan, today at 8:25 AM Eastern Time."

"Where is she headed now?"

"Toward Gary, Indiana."

She stops in Hornell, NY at 2:10 PM to refuel her plane

She stops for the night in Binghamton, NY at 4:20 PM

Miss Law arrives at Governors Island Nov. 20th at 9:37 AM

Vermilion, OH: November 19, 1916

"As a resident of Vermilion, what do you think of Miss Law's flight?"

"I think you have to admire her '**pluck**' for daring to make such an attempt."

McKean, PA: November 19, 1916

"What do you think of Miss Law's attempt to make history?"

"I think it's great. I'm amazed that she seems to be achieving her goal. There have been hundreds of people out here just trying to catch a **glimpse of her plane.**"

Hornell, New York: November 19, 1916

"Miss Law, it is 2:10 PM. What happened? Why did you land in Hornell?"

"I had **calculated** that 53 gallons of gasoline would get me from Chicago to Hornell. I knew I would stop here. I had hoped there would be some favorable wind to help. There was none. Ten miles outside of Hornell, my fuel was nearly depleted. Two miles from Hornell, I ran out completely. My engine quit, and I had to **glide** the final two miles to my landing site."

"Are you okay?"

"I am cold. My limbs are so numb they are not working well. I may need a little assistance to get to the automobile."

"Are you giving up?"

"No, I'm just going to get some food, replenish my gasoline, and have my machine filled with oil."

"Are you surprised at all the spectators that are here to see you?"

"A little, but I appreciate their encouragement."

"Are you helping with Miss Law's plane?"

"Yes."

"What time did she take off from Hornell?"

"At 3:24 PM. She's still headed for New York City."

"Does she know she's set a record? She flew 590 miles without a stop—averaging about 103 miles per hour. It's a new American cross-country distance record. No one in the United States has flown further. She's smashed the existing cross-country distance record of 452 miles, and she's broken the world's record for continuous flight for women pilots."

"I just hope she is okay. She had a close shave on takeoff and very nearly wrecked. See that huge hill toward the east—the one that's covered with the tall trees. It's about 600 feet high. She climbed as steeply as she could, but she nearly collided with those trees. The tops of the branches were practically striking the bottom of her plane."

Binghamton, NY: November 19, 1916

"Miss Law, it's 4:20 PM! Miss Law, why did you land in Binghamton?"

"It was getting dark, and I have no lights on my plane. I couldn't see my compass or any of my instruments."

"When we saw your plane, it stood out against the red, setting sun as clear cut as a **cameo**. Hundreds of people have been trying to get a glimpse of you. What are you going to do? Are you giving up?"

"No, I'm not giving up. I'm going to tie my plane to that tree and get a policeman to watch it during the night. I'll take off again in the morning."

Governors Island, NY: November 20, 1916

"Welcome to the aviation field at Governors Island, Miss Law. What time did you leave Binghamton? How was your flight?"

"I left at 7:23 AM. The fog was so thick that I could not see any landmarks. It was difficult to determine where I was going, but I finally picked up the Susquehanna River and then I followed the Delaware River to Port Jervis. I passed over Greenwood Lake, the Ramapo Mountains, and then I saw the Hudson River. I flew down the Hudson till I reached upper Manhattan, but my engine began to cut out and miss. My fuel supply was low. I had to tip the plane and then straighten out again to get the fuel to flow to the **carburetors**. I had to **volplane** for the last three miles of the flight and glide down with the wind instead of against it, but I made it."

"You landed at 9:37:35 AM. That means your total flight time for the 884 miles from Chicago to New York was 8 hours 55 minutes and 35 seconds. Congratulations, you made it to New York City. Yesterday you broke the American cross-country and nonstop record, and you've broken the world's record for continuous flight for women pilots. Listen to that cheering crowd and the bands playing. See all the dignitaries that have turned out to greet you. You've done it, Miss Law—it's the greatest flight ever made in America!"

"Victor Carlstrom! Mr. Carlstrom, can you tell our newspaper readers how you feel about Miss Law's flight? In setting a new American record for a distance flight, she has broken your record, and you used a modern 200-horsepower Curtiss military biplane. Your plane was more than twice as wide and high as Miss Law's plane and yours carried 200 gallons of gasoline."

"I have nothing but praise for Miss Law's accomplishment. She deserves great credit for her flight. It is the greatest performance of the year. Miss Law is one of the nerviest fliers in the business, but I have to admit that initially no one thought she would make any distance, much less break the record. People definitely doubted her abilities, but she has proven herself to be one of the great aviators."

Victor Carlstrom

New York City, New York: November 21, 1916

"Miss Law, the Aero Club of America made it official today. They've named you the record holder for the American nonstop cross-country flight. You have made the longest flight a woman ever made, haven't you?"

"I have made the longest flight an American ever made."

"Are you happy to have the record?"

"I'm happy that I made the flight, but I'm not boasting. I only undertook the flight to prove that it is an easy thing to fly from Chicago to New York. All one needs is an aircraft that can carry enough fuel for the journey. Now people will realize that both the mail and people can be timely transported between cities separated by hundreds of miles. I predict that in the future many people will fly from Chicago to New York for both business and pleasure. If an airplane has **sufficient** gasoline, there is no reason it cannot fly nonstop from Chicago to New York. If my gasoline had held out, I am confident I could have flown all the way from Chicago to New York City without making a stop."

New York City, New York: December 3, 1916

"Miss Law, you've become a national hero. You're the Queen of the Air. Your flight is more than a record. It has inspired the nation. You even got to meet President Woodrow Wilson, didn't you?"

Ruth Law meeting President Wilson

"Yes, he congratulated me and told me I was a great little flier."

"Has that been the highlight of your trip to New York City?"

"Well, I definitely enjoyed seeing the President, and I enjoyed being part of the ceremonies to illuminate the Statue of Liberty for the first time. I got to fly around Liberty's torch in a fiery airplane that spelled out the message 'Liberty.' It was great to be able to delight the thousands of people who were present, but I think, for me, the highlight of my trip has been the admiration and praise I have received from young girls."

"What girls?"

"School girls who have written me letters. One young girl, Esther Silverman, wrote to me and said: 'Now, I am glad I am a girl, because

PART SIX
DAILY NEWS

The Gazette News

SUNDAY
DECEMBER 10, 1916

STATUE OF LIBERTY ILLUMINATED!

LADY LIBERTY LIGHTS THE NIGHT IN GRAND SPECTACLE

The night was highlighted by the appearance of President Wilson, as well as Miss Ruth Law, the Chicago-to-New York record-breaking flyer, whose aeroplane flew across the night sky with a blaze of magnesium flame. Beneath her aeroplane, the word "L-I-B-E-R-T-Y" radiated in the darkness. Other highlights included two U.S. battleships anchored off the Battery, which were illuminated in

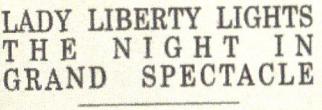

girls can do just as wonderful things as men. I am dreaming of the day when I may come to see you fly.' Another girl, Anna Rosenberg, said in her letter, 'You have made me feel that I may be proud to be a girl'."

"You enjoy being a role model for young girls?"

"I enjoy challenging the **stereotypes** regarding women—especially when it comes to flying. Women can be just as good pilots as men because they are courageous, self-possessed, and clear-headed. They are quick to decide in an emergency, and I think they usually make wise decisions. They are good aviators, and I believe there will be many female pilots in the future."

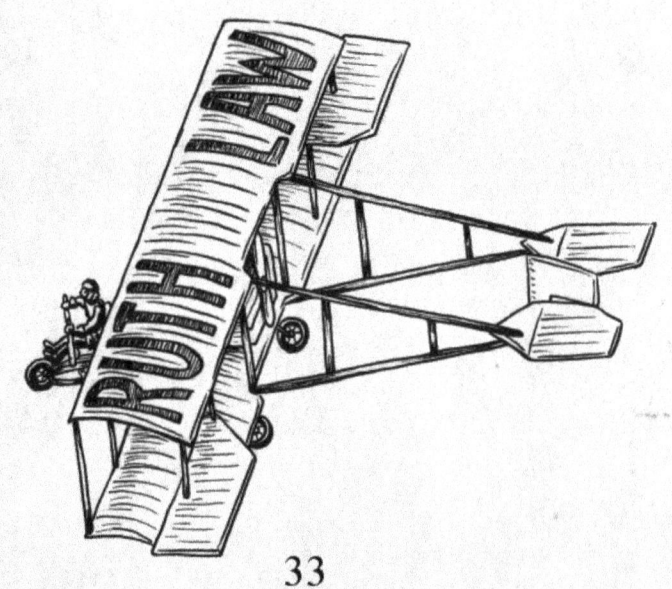

Ruth Bancroft Law (1887-1970)

Courtesy of the Smithsonian National Air and Space Museum (NASM A-5532)

Ruth Law was one of the best and most courageous aviators of her time. A remarkable pioneer who challenged stereotypes and established new aviation records, she was an excellent spokesman for pilots and a strong promoter of female aviators. She encouraged others to share her passion for flying and her vision for the future of aviation.

During World War I, Miss Law wore a regulation army aviation uniform and was billed as "Uncle Sam's only woman aviator." She promoted the war effort by dropping Liberty Loan bond "bombs" from her plane. After the war, she organized and starred in a barnstorming flying circus where she thrilled crowds with her aerial acrobatics. She also carried the first official air mail to the Philippine Islands.

Simply put, Miss Law said: "I fly because I like to." She once told *The Christian Science Monitor*: "There is an indescribable feeling which one experiences in flying; it comes with no other form of sport or navigation. It takes courage and daring; and one must be self-possessed, for there are moments when one's wits are tested to the full. Yet there is an exhilaration that compensates for all one's efforts."

It was on November 19, 1916, however, that Miss Law achieved her greatest feat. She didn't make it to New York City in one day, but she did establish a new cross-country distance record by flying from Chicago to Hornell, NY. In the process, she became the holder of the American record for a distance flight. Her achievement was astounding and amazing, but *how* she did it, in her little, obsolete "pusher" plane, was truly remarkable.

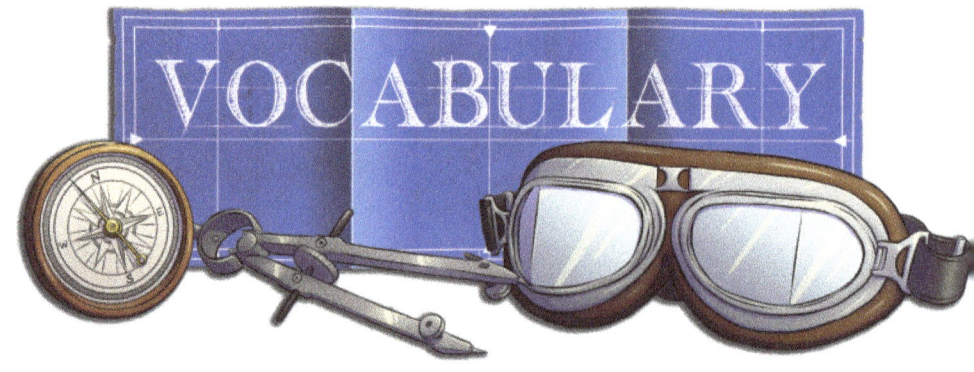

acrobatic - skillful changes in position, difficult and dangerous movements

altitude - height, the height of a plane above the ground

antiquated - old, old fashioned

attire - clothes, clothing

calculated - figured, planned

cameo - an object or a portrait, usually in profile, that stands out in relation to a background usually of different color

capacity - the largest amount something can hold or contain

carburetors - device/devices in an engine for mixing air with fuel so it can burn and provide power

catastrophe - disaster, tragedy

elements - weather conditions-such as cold winds and pouring rain

endurance - ability to withstand something- especially if it is hard or stressful

erratic - changing, unpredictable, inconsistent, not an even or regular pattern

fatigue - very tired, feelings of being tired

gale - strong wind

gauntlet - a long glove

glide - an unpowered flight

maneuvers - skilled movements

manufacturer - a person or a company that makes something - such as an airplane

obsolete - out of date, no longer used

pluck - daring, courage, bravery, spirit

practicality - workability, reasonableness

rudders - moveable flat pieces of wood or metal attached at the rear of a plane that aid steering

sanctioned - approved, permitted

stamina - ability to sustain lengthy physical or mental effort, staying power

stereotypes - widely-held ideas or beliefs about a person or group of people that may be too simple, unfair, and untrue

sufficient - enough, adequate

surplus - extra, unneeded, unwanted

throttle - device for controlling or regulating the flow of fuel to an engine

tumult - commotion, frenzy

vertical - being aligned at a right angle to the horizon, up and down position from the ground

volplane - make a controlled downward flight in an airplane with the engine off, a dive with no engine power

- Ruth Law's plane used 53 gallons of gasoline for her flight from Chicago to Hornell (~590 miles), averaging approximately 11 miles per gallon of fuel.

- Ruth Law made numerous flights for competitions, exhibitions, and to carry passengers. In 1914, she set a world's record for passenger carrying by a woman. She took two passengers aloft for ten minutes flying at about 800 feet.

- Rodman Law, Ruth Law's brother, was known as the "human fly" for his daring exploits. He climbed many high buildings with his bare hands and parachuted from balloons and planes.

- A remarkable stunt and exhibition flier, Ruth Law flew between tall buildings, through cascading fireworks, raced low against motor cars on the ground, and walked across the wings of high-flying aircraft. In one aerial stunt, she was known for climbing out of the cockpit, walking to the center of the wings of the airplane, and standing upright while the pilot flew the plane through consecutive loops.

- Ruth Law stopped flying around 1922. Her husband, Charles Oliver, is believed to have persuaded her to stop out of concerns for her safety.

- Ruth Law's prediction that many people would fly from Chicago to New York for business and pleasure proved accurate. As one of the busiest air routes in the United States, flights between Chicago and New York carry millions of passengers each year.

SOURCE NOTES

Chicago, Illinois: November 18, 1916--
Page 2, lines 5-9: "Will Try To Fly Here: Woman Aviator to Attempt to Break Carlstrom's Records." *New York Times*, 17 Nov. 1916, 16.
Page 2, line 16: "She Holds Other Records: Won Altitude Competition for Women—Has Been Licensed 4 Years." *New York Times*, 20 Nov. 1916, 4.
Page 2, line 17: "Pilot Stories: Ruth Law." Smithsonian National Postal Museum, 2004. Available: http://www.postalmuseum.si.edu/airmail/pilot/pilot_female/pilot_female_law.html.
Page 3, line 3: "She Holds Other Records," *NYT*, 20 Nov. 1916, 4.
Page 4, lines 1-3: "Will Try To Fly Here," *NYT*, 17 Nov. 1916, 16.
Page 4, lines 16-18: "Ruth Law Lands Here From Chicago in Record Flight: Gasoline Nearly Gone on Last Leg of Her Journey, She Volplanes to Governors Island. Glides Through Dense Fog, Gen. Wood Greets Her at End of 884-Mile Trip, Made in 8 Hours, 55 Min., 35 Sec., Almost Benumbed by Cold, Trip Hailed as America's Greatest Flight—Will Try Again with a Big Machine." *New York Times*, 21 Nov. 1916, 1 + 3.
Page 6, lines 2-3: Ruth Law. "Miss Law Tells of Her Record Flight; To Try Non-Stop New York Trip Next: Proud That She Has Beaten Carlstrom's Recent Record and Has Done So In a Small and Old Machine With Limited Fuel Capacity." *New York Times*, 20 Nov. 1916, 1 + 4.
Page 6, lines 3-4: "Ruth Law Lands Here," *NYT*, 21 Nov. 1916, 3.
Page 6, lines 6-10: "Noted Aviatrix Says She Likes to Fly Because Other Girls Can't." *Joplin Globe* (Joplin, MO), 13 June 1917, 2; Law, "Miss Law Tells of Her Record Flight," *NYT*, 20 Nov. 1916, 1, and "A Woman Flies 590 Miles." *New York Times*, 20 Nov. 1916, 12.
Page 7, lines 1-5: "Noted Aviatrix," *Joplin Globe*, 13 June 1917, 2, and "Ruth Law Lands Here," *NYT*, 21 Nov. 1916, 1.
Page 7, lines 8-10: "Noted Aviatrix," *Joplin Globe*, 13 June 1917, 2.
Page 7, lines 12-15: "Noted Aviatrix," *Joplin Globe*, 13 June 1917, 2.
Page 8, lines 3-9; page 9, lines 1-3: Emily Watson. "Not Afraid: Daredevil Ruth Law Almost Forced to First Fly Plane." *Sarasota Journal*, 6 Nov. 1958, 19, and "The Record Made Official." *New York Times*, 21 Nov. 1916, 3.
Page 9, lines 5-6: "Noted Aviatrix," *Joplin Globe*, 13 June 1917, 2.
Page 9, lines 7-9; page 10, lines 1-2: "Noted Aviatrix," *Joplin Globe*, 13 June 1917, 2.
Page 10, lines 8-13: Law, "Miss Law Tells of Her Record Flight," *NYT*, 20 Nov. 1916, 1.
Page 10, lines 17-18; page 12, line 1: "Starts in Gusty Half Gale: Miss Law Sails Away Toward Indiana Only 200 Feet in the Air." *New York Times*, 20 Nov. 1916, 4.
Page 12, lines 4-6; page 13, lines 1-3: Law, "Miss Law Tells of Her Record Flight," *NYT*, 20 Nov. 1916, 1 + 4.
Page 13, lines 6-9: Law, "Miss Law Tells of Her Record Flight," *NYT*, 20 Nov. 1916, 1.
Page 13, lines 16-17: "Ruth Law Lands Here," *NYT*, 21 Nov. 1916, 3.

Chicago, Illinois: November 19, 1916--
Page 15, lines 2-5: Law, "Miss Law Tells of Her Record Flight," *NYT*, 20 Nov. 1916, 1, and "Starts in Gusty Half Gale," *NYT*, 20 Nov. 1916, 4.
Page 16, lines 1-3: "Starts in Gusty Half Gale," *NYT*, 20 Nov. 1916, 4.
Page 16, lines 5-11: "Starts in Gusty Half Gale," *NYT*, 20 Nov. 1916, 4.
Page 16, lines 14-16: "Ruth Law Flies 590 Miles Without Stop; Beats Both Victor Carlstrom's Records; Due to Reach New York at 9 A. M. Today. Down for Lack of Fuel: Makes Remarkable Trip in Obsolete Machine in Use Two Years. Her First Distance Effort: Travels Without a Hitch at 103 Miles an Hour Till Supply of Gasoline Is Exhausted. World's Woman Record: Gets Away from Chicago in Gusty Wind—Aviators Are Amazed by Performance." *New York Times*, 20 Nov. 1916, 1 + 4.

Vermilion, OH: November 19, 1916--
Page 19, lines 1-5: "Ruth Law Flies 590 Miles," *NYT*, 20 Nov. 1916, 1.

McKean, PA: November 19, 1916--
Page 19, lines 6-10: "Ruth Law Flies 590 Miles," *NYT*, 20 Nov. 1916, 1.

Hornell, New York: November 19, 1916--
Page 20, lines 4-11: Law, "Miss Law Tells of Her Record Flight," *NYT*, 20 Nov. 1916, 1.
Page 20, lines 13-15: "Lifted From Her Craft: Miss Law So Benumbed at Hornell That Men Assisted Her to Auto." *New York Times*, 20 Nov. 1916, 4.
Page 20, lines 17-18; page 21, line 1: "Lifted From Her Craft," *NYT*, 20 Nov. 1916, 4.
Page 22, lines 1-11: "Ruth Law Flies 590 Miles," *NYT*, 20 Nov. 1916, 1.
Page 22, lines 12-18: Law, "Miss Law Tells of Her Record Flight," *NYT*, 20 Nov. 1916, 4.
Binghamton, New York: November 19, 1916--
Page 24, lines 4-6: Law, "Miss Law Tells of Her Record Flight," *NYT*, 20 Nov. 1916, 1.
Page 24, lines 7-9: "A Cameo in the Setting Sun: All Binghamton Out to See Miss Law Sweep in from the West." *New York Times*, 20 Nov. 1916, 4.
Page 24, lines 12-15: Law, "Miss Law Tells of Her Record Flight," *NYT*, 20 Nov. 1916, 4.
Governors Island, New York: November 20, 1916--
Page 25, lines 5-18: "Ruth Law Lands Here," *NYT*, 21 Nov. 1916, 1 + 3.
Page 26, lines 1-9; page 27, lines 1-2: "Ruth Law Lands Here," *NYT*, 21 Nov. 1916, 1 + 3.
Page 27, lines 5-9; page 28, line 1: "Ruth Law Lands Here," *NYT*, 21 Nov. 1916, 3, and "Ruth Law Flies 590 Miles," *NYT*, 20 Nov. 1916, 1.
Page 28, lines 2-10: "Finest Feat of Year, Carlstrom's Opinion: Says Miss Law Has Set Mark for Men Aviators—Calls Her 'One of Nerviest Fliers'." *New York Times*, 20 November 1916, 4, and "Topics of the Times: An Aviator Is She In Reality." *New York Times*, 21 Nov. 1916, 10.
New York City, New York: November 21, 1916--
Page 29, lines 2-5: "The Record Made Official." *NYT*, 21 Nov. 1916, 3.
Page 29, lines 5-8: "Ruth Law Lands Here," *NYT*, 21 Nov. 1916, 1.
Page 29, lines 10-18; page 30, lines 1-6: Law, "Miss Law Tells of Her Record Flight," *NYT*, 20 Nov. 1916, 1 + 4, "Ruth Law Lands Here," *NYT*, 21 Nov. 1916, 3, and "Ruth Law Flies 590 Miles," *NYT*, 20 Nov. 1916, 1.
New York City, New York: December 3, 1916--
Page 31, lines 1-2: "Peace Can Come Only With Liberty, Not While Destinies are Ruled by Small Selfish Groups, Says Wilson: Cheers Greet Sentiment, President by Inference Picks France for Special Favor, Says We Have Same Ideals, Diners in Honor of Liberty Light Give Ovation to Message from Poincare, Wilson Greets Ruth Law." *New York Times*, 3 Dec. 1916: 1 + 2.
Page 31, lines 6-10: "Miss Law to Circle Statue of Liberty: Aviatrice Who Made Flight from Chicago Will Help Dedicate Lighting Plant. She Won't Do Any 'Stunts,' Her Aeroplane Will Carry Electric Lights and Magnesium Torches." *New York Times*, 30 Nov. 1916: 5, and "Signal by the President Bathes Liberty Statue in Flood of Light: Throngs See Dedication of Illuminating Plant—Warships Boom Salute, While Ruth Law Soars in Fiery Aeroplane about Liberty's Torch." *New York Times*, 3 Dec. 1916: 1 + 2.
Page 31, lines 17-18; page 32, lines 1-3, page 33, lines 1-2: "Ruth Law the Idol of Boys and Girls: Fifty Pupils of Brooklyn School 83 Write Individual Letters of Congratulation, Girls Proud of Her Flight, Boys Generously Chivalrous and Hopeful that They May Some Day Be Aviators." *New York Times*, 26 Nov. 1916, 14.
Page 33, lines 7-12: "Women as Aviators." *The Christian Science Monitor*, 26 May 1917, 22.
Ruth Bancroft Law (1887-1970)
Page 36, lines 3-5: "Ruth Law Thrills Crowd That Greets Flight in City." *Joplin Globe*, 13 June 1917: 1, and "Ruth Law Now Due Here This Morning: Famous Aviatrix Encounters Severe Kansas Windstorm and Is Delayed." *Joplin Globe*, 12 June 1917, 2.
Page 36, lines 5-7: "Ruth Law, in Sensational Flight, Beats Rainstorm." *Joplin Globe*, 9 June 1917, 1, and "Ruth Law, Famous Flier, to Bombard Joplin Monday Morning." *Joplin Globe*, 10 June 1917, 13.
Page 36, lines 7-9: Watson, "Not Afraid," *Sarasota Journal*, 6 Nov. 1958, 19.
Page 36, lines 9-10: "Pilot Stories: Ruth Law." Smithsonian National Postal Museum, 2004. Available: http://www.postalmuseum.si.edu/airmail/pilot/pilot_female/pilot_female_law.html.
Page 36, lines 11-12: "Noted Aviatrix," *Joplin Globe*, 13 June 1917, 2.
Page 36, lines 12-18: "Women as Aviators." *The Christian Science Monitor*, 26 May 1917, 22.

This account of Miss Law's historic feat is based on newspaper reports and articles published at the time of her flight that recorded her story. Her own words and those of others cited at the time have been used frequently to augment the authenticity of this account. Check out the sources below to learn more about Miss Law, the original accounts of her flight, and her remarkable achievement.

References
Used to Tell the Story of *Ruth Law—The Queen of the Air*

"A Cameo in the Setting Sun: All Binghamton Out to See Miss Law Sweep in from the West." *New York Times*, 20 Nov. 1916, 4.

"A Woman Flies 590 Miles." *New York Times*, 20 Nov. 1916: 12.

"Finest Feat of Year, Carlstrom's Opinion: Says Miss Law Has Set Mark for Men Aviators—Calls Her 'One of Nerviest Fliers'." *New York Times*, 20 November 1916, 4.

Law, Ruth. "Miss Law Tells of Her Record Flight; To Try Non-Stop New York Trip Next: Proud That She Has Beaten Carlstrom's Recent Record and Has Done So In a Small and Old Machine With Limited Fuel Capacity." *New York Times*, 20 Nov. 1916: 1 + 4.

"Lifted From Her Craft: Miss Law So Benumbed at Hornell That Men Assisted Her to Auto." *New York Times*, 20 Nov. 1916, 4.

"Miss Law to Circle Statue of Liberty: Aviatrice Who Made Flight from Chicago Will Help Dedicate Lighting Plant. She Won't Do Any 'Stunts,' Her Aeroplane Will Carry Electric Lights and Magnesium Torches." *New York Times*, 30 Nov. 1916: 5.

"Noted Aviatrix Says She Likes to Fly Because Other Girls Can't." *Joplin Globe* (Joplin, MO), 13 June 1917, 2.

"Peace Can Come Only With Liberty, Not While Destinies are Ruled by Small Selfish Groups, Says Wilson: Cheers Greet Sentiment, President by Inference Picks France for Special Favor, Says We Have Same Ideals, Diners in Honor of Liberty Light Give Ovation to Message from Poincare, Wilson Greets Ruth Law." *New York Times*, 3 Dec. 1916: 1 + 2.

"Pilot Stories: Ruth Law." Smithsonian National Postal Museum, 2004. Available from: http://www.postalmuseum.si.edu/airmail/pilot/pilot_female/pilot_female_law.html.

"Ruth Law, Famous Flier, to Bombard Joplin Monday Morning." *Joplin Globe* (Joplin, MO), 10 June 1917, 13.

"Ruth Law Flies 590 Miles Without Stop; Beats Both Victor Carlstrom's Records; Due to Reach New York at 9 A. M. Today. Down for Lack of Fuel: Makes Remarkable Trip in Obsolete Machine in Use Two Years. Her First Distance Effort: Travels Without a Hitch at 103 Miles an Hour Till Supply of Gasoline Is Exhausted. World's Woman Record: Gets Away from Chicago in Gusty Wind—Aviators Are Amazed by Performance." *New York Times*, 20 Nov. 1916, 1 + 4.

"Ruth Law, in Sensational Flight, Beats Rainstorm." *Joplin Globe* (Joplin, MO), 9 June 1917, 1.

"Ruth Law Lands Here From Chicago in Record Flight: Gasoline Nearly Gone on Last Leg of Her Journey, She Volplanes to Governors Island. Glides Through Dense Fog, Gen. Wood Greets Her at End of 884-Mile Trip, Made in 8 Hours, 55 Min., 35 Sec., Almost Benumbed by Cold, Trip Hailed as America's Greatest Flight—Will Try Again with a Big Machine." *New York Times*, 21 Nov. 1916: 1 + 3.

"Ruth Law Now Due Here This Morning: Famous Aviatrix Encounters Severe Kansas Windstorm and Is Delayed." *Joplin Globe* (Joplin, MO), 12 June 1917, 2.

"Ruth Law the Idol of Boys and Girls: Fifty Pupils of Brooklyn School 83 Write Individual Letters of Congratulation, Girls Proud of Her Flight, Boys Generously Chivalrous and Hopeful that They May Some Day Be Aviators." *New York Times*, 26 Nov. 1916: 14.

"Ruth Law Thrills Crowd That Greets Flight in City." *Joplin Globe* (Joplin, MO), 13 June 1917: 1.

"She Holds Other Records: Won Altitude Competition for Women—Has Been Licensed 4 Years." *New York Times*, 20 Nov. 1916, 4.

"Signal by the President Bathes Liberty Statue in Flood of Light: Throngs See Dedication of Illuminating Plant—Warships Boom Salute, While Ruth Law Soars in Fiery Aeroplane about Liberty's Torch." *New York Times*, 3 Dec. 1916: 1 + 2.

"Starts in Gusty Half Gale: Miss Law Sails Away Toward Indiana Only 200 Feet in the Air." *New York Times*, 20 Nov. 1916, 4.

"The Record Made Official." *New York Times*, 21 Nov. 1916, 3.

"Topics of the Times: An Aviator Is She In Reality." *New York Times*, 21 Nov. 1916: 10.

Watson, Emily. "Not Afraid: Daredevil Ruth Law Almost Forced to First Fly Plane." *Sarasota Journal*, 6 Nov. 1958, 19.

"Will Try To Fly Here: Woman Aviator to Attempt to Break Carlstrom's Records." *New York Times*, 17 Nov. 1916: 16.

"Women as Aviators." *The Christian Science Monitor*, 26 May 1917, 22.

ADDITIONAL BOOKS YOU MAY ENJOY
by
Billie Holladay Skelley

Luella Agnes Owen: Going Where No Lady Had Gone Before
Crossing Time Series-Book 1

Ruth Law: The Queen of the Air
Crossing Time Series-Book 2

Hugh Armstrong Robinson: The Story of Flying Lucky 13
Crossing Time Series-Book 3

Hypatia: Ancient Alexandria's Female Scholar
Crossing Time Series-Book 4

Eagle the Legal Beagle

Ollie the Autism-Support Collie

Weaver the Diabetic-Alert Retriever

Spice Secret: A Cautionary Diary

Two Terrible Days in May: The Rader Farm Massacre

It's Almost Time to Celebrate St. Patrick's Day

Tapeti: The Moon's Keeper

www.ingramcontent.com/pod-product-compliance
Lightning Source LLC
Chambersburg PA
CBHW050731010526
44107CB00009B/806